The Virginia Carroll Crawford Collection
AMERICAN DECORATIVE ARTS, 1825-1917

Copyright 1983
High Museum of Art.
All rights reserved.
Published by the High Museum
of Art, Atlanta, Georgia.

Edited by Kelly Morris
Designed by Jim Zambounis
Printed by Preston Rose
Company, Atlanta

Library of Congress
Catalogue No. 83-81102
ISBN 0-939802-16-3

Front cover: Central panel from
    Herter Brothers cabinet,
    ca. 1880 (see page 54)
Back cover: Elevator grille from
    Chicago Stock Exchange,
    designed by Louis Sullivan,
    ca. 1893-94 (see page 80)
Inside covers: Adapted from an
    1870s upholstery fabric

Photo Credits:
David Behl, New York City:
    pages 19, 30, 56, 62, 94
Richard Goodbody, New York
    City: pages 26, 27, 38, 44, 75,
    79, 83, 85, 86, 87, 89, 93, 94
Helga Photo Studio, Upper
    Montclair, New Jersey: front
    cover, pages 16, 17, 20, 21,
    23, 24, 25, 31, 33, 36, 37, 39,
    40, 41, 42, 43, 45, 46, 47, 50,
    51, 53, 54, 57, 58, 60, 61, 64,
    65, 68, 69, 70, 71, 72, 73, 76,
    82, 83, 84, 85, 86, 87, 88, 89,
    90, 91, 92, 93, 94
Schreter Me Sun Lee, New York
    City: pages 15, 29, 74, 81
Michael McKelvey, Atlanta:
    pages 15, 48, 49, 59, 66, 67,
    77, 82, 83, 87, 88, 91
David Parker, Brooklyn: 29, 81
Mary Carolyn Pindar, Atlanta:
    page 4
Courtesy Sagamore Hill National
    Historic Site: page 78
Courtesy Sotheby's, New York
    City: page 52
Jerry L. Thompson, New York
    City: pages 22, 34, 35, 55, 63,
    80, back cover

The Virginia Carroll Crawford Collection
AMERICAN DECORATIVE ARTS, 1825-1917

David A. Hanks and Donald C. Peirce

High Museum of Art
Atlanta, Georgia

Virginia Carroll Crawford

Acknowledgments

The talents and skills of many individuals have been contributed to the Crawford project. As Director of the Museum, Gudmund Vigtel has lent his enthusiasm, support, and advice. Katharine Gross Farnham, Curator of Decorative Arts when collecting began, first envisioned the project's possibilities. Catherine Lynn developed the concept into a program for collecting. Caroline Stern and Derek Ostergard of David A. Hanks and Associates, and Elizabeth Bacchetti, Assistant to the Curator of Decorative Arts, deserve special recognition for their tireless efforts in organizing details of photography, conservation, and preparation of manuscripts for both catalogue and installation labels. Shelby White Cave managed the move of the collection from the New York warehouses to the new Museum in Atlanta. Kelly Morris ably edited the manuscript, and Jim Zambounis designed the handsome catalogue. Besides the staff of the High Museum, many others have assisted in the development of the collection. These include Hope Alswang, Arthur Andersen & Co., Lee B. Anderson, Charles Anello, Dea Bacchetti, Susan Berman, Charles E. Buckley, Mrs. Emory Cocke, Rudolph Colban, Margaret B. Caldwell, Stiles Tuttle Colwill, Angela D'Antuono, Sam Dornsife, Martin Eidelberg, Donald Fennimore, Roy Frangiamore, Richard Goodbody, James M. Goode, Mrs. Richard Graham, Richard H. Howland, Marilynn Johnson, Hermes Knauer, Richard McGeehan, Mark Meachen, Robert Mehlman, R. Craig Miller, Dianne H. Pilgrim, Debe Quevis, Lynn Springer Roberts, Rodris Roth, Wilmot and Arlene Palmer Schwind, Kevin Stayton, Gary and Diana Stradling, Irma Strauss, Peter L. L. Strickland, Page Talbott, Arthur Vitols, Robert Walker, Gregory Weidman, and Philip White. Of course, the greatest appreciation goes to a most generous benefactor, Virginia Carroll Crawford.

D.A.H. and D.C.P.

Preface

It was a happy coincidence that brought together a generous friend and trustee, Virginia Carroll Crawford, and Catherine Lynn's 1978 recommendation that the High Museum collect American decorative arts of the 19th and early 20th centuries. Few art museums were then systematically collecting post-Federal decorative arts. Objects from that period were still unfashionable, hence plentiful and relatively affordable. The opportunity for a bold and meaningful collection was clear and Virginia Crawford responded without hesitation.

The collection was begun under the curatorship of Katharine Farnham, who was aided by the expertise of David A. Hanks. Mr. Hanks had worked with the High Museum's staff previously, with his exhibition *The Decorative Designs of Frank Lloyd Wright*, which had travelled to several American museums in the late 1970s. His extensive museum experience and his understanding of post-Federal design made him a highly effective consultant to the Museum and Virginia Crawford in this undertaking.

In the spring of 1980, Donald C. Peirce was appointed the High Museum's first full-time Curator of Decorative Arts and the Crawford Collection has grown significantly under his guidance. The result of this fortuitous collaboration among benefactor, museum staff, and consultant is a collection of consistently high quality of design and extraordinary craftsmanship, of great stylistic breadth, full of delightful surprises.

Perhaps the most persuasive factor in Mrs. Crawford's commitment was the importance of such a collection to the study of decorative design in America, for this group of objects serves as a link between early American styles and modern forms. There is no doubt that the Crawford Collection puts the High Museum in the forefront in this period. The Museum's presentation of this important material has been given special emphasis by the brilliant installation by Richard Meier in a particularly successful integration of object and environment.

Virginia Crawford's support of this daring project will clearly have a far-reaching impact on the High Museum as well as on American scholarship. We are deeply grateful to her for her faith in the staff's judgments. Her dedicated support is an outstanding example of enlightened museum benefaction.

Gudmund Vigtel
Director

Foreword

With the unveiling of the Virginia Carroll Crawford Collection on the occasion of the opening of the new High Museum of Art, it may seem to many visitors that the Museum has acquired a major collection overnight. In fact, the collection as it now exists is the result of a decade of planning and four years of intensive effort.

Ten years ago, the High Museum had a strong interest in decorative arts but its collections were small. Mr. and Mrs. Emory Cocke had just established what has become a fine representation of English ceramics for the Museum. An anonymous grant made possible a core collection of 18th and early 19th century American furniture, but it was apparent that growth in this field would be slow. Katharine Gross Farnham, then Curator of Decorative Arts, considered other ways in which the Museum might make significant acquisitions. One suggestion was a stylistic survey of chairs, which often illustrate subtle evolutions in style. However, the vision of furniture galleries repeating the same form seemed monotonous and the idea was abandoned.

Many felt that the Museum, a southern institution, should be a center for the study and exhibition of regional decorative arts. The Museum has responded to this view by presenting southern exhibitions and collections of the best quality. But furniture made in the South is relatively scarce, and aggressive collecting has rapidly reduced its availability. Had the Museum pursued this field of decorative arts as its main sphere of activity, the presentations would have been limited.

By the late 1970s, a growing group of Atlanta collectors, designers, and architects were studying the decorative arts of the 19th and 20th centuries. This interest was vividly demonstrated at the Museum when a group called The Friends for a Frank Lloyd

Wright Exhibition was organized to raise funds which enabled the Museum to present *The Decorative Designs of Frank Lloyd Wright* in 1979. The exhibition was exceedingly popular, and, by the end of its showing, plans were already underway for the 1980 presentation of *A Thing of Beauty: Art Nouveau, Art Deco, Arts & Crafts Movement and Aesthetic Movement Objects in Atlanta Collections.*

In light of this enthusiastic interest, Katharine Farnham identified an area of collecting where the High Museum of Art might concentrate and excel. In the summer of 1978, Catherine Lynn, former Curator at the Atlanta Historical Society and Ph.D. candidate at Yale University, was appointed to a summer research position at the Museum. Her major assignment was to develop a program for the High Museum's collecting of 19th century American decorative arts.

The report was extensive and detailed. It not only gave a history of 19th century design and art theory, but also clearly outlined the practicalities of the Museum's pursuing this area of collecting. By 1979, the range of available 17th century and 18th century material was small, whereas works of comparable craftsmanship from the 19th century were relatively abundant. Also, objects documented to owners and makers survived in far greater numbers from the 19th century than from the earlier period.

The idea of collecting and presenting 19th century material was not entirely new among American art museums—the Philadelphia Museum of Art pioneered with an exhibition of 19th century objects in 1933, followed by The Brooklyn Museum's *Victoriana* in 1960, and The Metropolitan Museum of Art's monumental *19th Century America: Furniture and Other Decorative Arts* in 1970—but no art museum had been able to implement an organized program of collecting 19th century decorative arts. (The Margaret Woodbury Strong Museum in Rochester, NY, has collected 19th century American objects presented in cultural, social, and historical contexts.) A few discerning collectors and museum curators who could persuade donors to acquire objects beyond the traditional 1840 cutoff date were attempting to expand into this area. But these were exceptions. When the report was completed, it was filed with other possible programs, and a copy was submitted to the Director of the Museum.

At about the same time, Virginia Carroll Crawford approached the Director with the idea of supporting a collection which would be developed in a short period of time and would culminate in a special exhibition and catalogue. A Board member and generous patron of the Museum, Mrs. Crawford had enabled the Museum to make a variety of acquisitions, including a desk and bookcase from Piedmont Georgia, a Federal painted worktable made in Salem, Massachusetts, and two paintings, *Camel's Hump* by John Kensett and *Supreme Hardware Store* by the 20th century artist Richard Estes. When shown the report's recommendation that the Museum develop a collection of 19th century American decorative arts, Mrs. Crawford was intrigued. Her immediate enthusiasm for this project reflected not only her faith in the Museum but also her longtime interest in the decorative arts.

Overseeing the Crawford project was such a monumental task—involving acquisitions, cataloguing, photography, and conservation—that a consulting curator, David A. Hanks, was employed to represent the Museum. At that time, the High Museum facility simply had no space for properly showing or storing the collection. Consequently, secure warehouse space in New York was leased for the storage of the objects and to serve as a staging area for Hanks in assembling the collection and preparing it for exhibition. Supervision of the Crawford Collection, and expanded activities in the decorative arts generally, required a full-time curator, and Donald C. Peirce joined the High Museum staff in 1980.

In May of 1979, Virginia Crawford, the High Museum, and the consulting curator embarked on a new venture in collecting, an unparalleled cooperative effort. In that month, Mrs. Crawford approved the acquisition of a music cabinet made by Thomas Godey in Baltimore between 1868 and 1872 (see page 31). This purchase established the procedure of acquiring for the collection: the Director, the consulting curator, and the Curator of Decorative Arts would reach an agreement and unanimously recommend objects for Mrs. Crawford's approval.

One of the great pleasures in working with a small collection, or starting a new collection, is that the addition of each object generates greater excitement than the filling of a gap in an already established and comprehensive collection. Developing a collection from its inception is an absorbing and tremendously satisfying experience for both the curator and collector. With the Crawford project, the thrill of seeking and discovering treasures was repeated over and over again.

Each new object represented a definition of the collection's goals, a fresh surge of energy. The first purchase was exemplary. The Godey cabinet, with its intricate marquetry and beautifully cast gilt bronze mounts, represents some of the finest craftsmanship of its period. The printed label affixed to the back of the cabinet identifies Thomas Godey as its maker, and gives his business address as 41 Hanover Street in Baltimore. According to Baltimore city directories,

Godey worked at this address between 1868 and 1872. Hence, the cabinet can be precisely associated with a particular time, place, and person, serving not only as a work of art, but also as an important historical document. The cabinet re-establishes the reputation of a major, if until recently forgotten, Baltimore maker. Acquisition of the Godey cabinet was an auspicious beginning.

Shortly after this purchase, an inlaid card table made by Alexander Roux of New York City between 1867 and 1877 (see page 29) was bought at auction. Because of the complexity of museum acquisition procedures, it is usually difficult for institutions to act quickly enough to participate in art auctions. With Mrs. Crawford's support, however, the High Museum was able to compete effectively in the private sector of art collecting.

Since 1979, 139 objects have been gathered for the Virginia Carroll Crawford Collection. Many consultants, curators, dealers, and institutions have participated in the development, conservation, and documentation of the Collection, and they are listed in the Acknowledgments. Of course, the ultimate credit is due to a remarkable benefactor, Virginia Carroll Crawford.

David A. Hanks
Consulting Curator

Donald C. Peirce
Curator of Decorative Arts

The Virginia Carroll Crawford Collection

Dimensions: height before width before depth

Classicism

For the first third of the 19th century, a single style permeated virtually every aspect of the arts in America. The attenuated lines of 18th century Neo-Classicism were abandoned for bold forms based on Greek and Roman precedents. The monumentality of early 19th century Classicism expressed the noble ideals of the young republic, and helped identify the new democracy with classical civilizations. The style was deemed appropriate not only for governmental structures but also for the dwellings of citizens. The style was rooted in Napoleonic France and was brought to America by French emigrant craftsmen. The reliance of American designers on Classical detail persisted through all of the eclectic "revivals" of the 19th century and remained an important aspect of American taste well into the 20th century.

Tea Service
Silver

Edward Lownes (1792-1834)
Philadelphia, ca. 1833
Teapot: 12 x 11¼ x 6¼ inches
Teapot: 11½ x 11⅛ x 6 inches
Sugar Bowl: 10½ x 9 x 9 inches
Creamer: 9⅛ x 7¼ x 4½ inches

1982.301.1 - 1982.301.4

The exuberant combination of Classical forms and Rococo decoration makes this four-piece set transitional in style.

Particularly noteworthy are the fine chased work and cast decoration. The beautiful calligraphy of the inscription reads: "PRESENTED TO JOHN SWIFT, ESQ. / by his Fellow Citizens / as a testimonial of their / Gratitude / for his services at the / Arch Street Prison / on Sunday August 5, 1832 / during the prevalence of the / MALIGNANT CHOLERA." John Swift (1790-1873), mayor of Philadelphia, was one of a group of citizens and physicians who risked infection and death to assist during the 1832 cholera epidemic. According to a contemporary account, "The committee of North Ward named as principal among the citizens, John Swift . . . [who] was taken sick the day after. He was conspicuous at the prison, and narrowly escaped death." This set was commissioned from Edward Lownes for a March 1833 presentation and is stamped "E. Lownes" on the pedestal feet.

Pair of Argand Lamps
Bronze, glass, gilt

Messenger & Sons, London and
Birmingham
Retailed by Jones, Lows & Ball
Company (listed in business
1839)
Boston, ca. 1839
25¾ x 19 x 8½ inches

1982.308.1, 1982.308.2

In 1783, Ami Argand, a Swiss
chemist, developed a lamp
designed on scientific principles
of combustion. A hollow tube
admitted air to the center of the
flame, increasing combustion; the
light was intensified by a glass
chimney. The Argand reservoir
was placed above the level of the
flame so that oil could flow to the
burner as needed. Argand lamps
were manufactured well into the
19th century. American

manufacturers or retailers of
Argand lamps were often silver
and jewelry merchants and
makers—e.g., Baldwin Gardiner
of New York, Christopher
Cornelius of Philadelphia, and
Jones, Lows & Ball, a
predecessor of Shreve, Crump
and Low of Boston.
Distinguished by fine quality and
monumental scale, each of the
lamps bears a metal plaque
marked, "MESSENGER &
SONS / LONDON &
BIRMINGHAM /
MANUFACTURED FOR /
JONES, LOWS & BALL /
BOSTON." It is unusual for the
manufacturer to be recorded in
this way. Such marks often give
only the retailer's name, as lamps
of this type were normally
imported in parts and assembled
in this county.

16

Pitcher
Porcelain, polychrome and gilt decoration

Tucker and Hemphill
(working 1826-1838)
Philadelphia, 1834
9⅜ x 7⅝ x 5¾ inches

VC-084

Functional decorative wares like this pitcher were produced by William Ellis Tucker's Philadelphia factory. Combining skilled painting, enameling, and gilding, the pitcher is typical of the best of Tucker's production. Tucker's son Thomas was chief factory designer and the decorator responsible for the polychrome floral designs. This pitcher, with the initials "J.C.L." in monogram and the date "1834," was owned by George Horace Lorimer of Philadelphia, an early collector of Americana.

Tucker and Hemphill succeeded in manufacturing superior grades of porcelain, frequently the equal of imported wares, from native Pennsylvania clays. However, because of low import tariffs, European wares could be sold at lower prices. In a letter written January 31, 1831, to a United States Senator, Tucker complained that lack of funds prevented his establishing a ceramic factory in the United States the equal of Sèvres in France. Unable to compete, the factory closed a year after the national bank failures of 1837.

Gothic and Elizabethan Revivals

In the first years of the American republic, Classical conventions dominated architecture and interior decoration among the wealthy. After 1830, however, many prominent members of American intellectual and artistic circles—including such influential architects and arbiters of taste as Alexander Jackson Davis and Andrew Jackson Downing—spurned Classical symmetry. The romantic pursuit of the picturesque, already prevalent in the arts and literature of England, began to be expressed in Gothic architecture and furnishings. Neither the Gothic Revival nor the Elizabethan Revival was embraced as widely by Americans as Classicism had been, but the impact of these models on the American environment was profound. Asymmetrical designs and somber palettes for both interior and exterior ornament were introduced. But Gothic furniture of the 19th century owed its appearance more to the reproduction of medieval details than forms; indeed, interest in detail over form was characteristic of this and subsequent 19th century revivals. The influence of Gothic and Elizabethan taste lasted for more than fifty years. By mid-century, however, the modern French taste, embodied in Rococo-inspired furniture, had been introduced, reaching its greatest popularity during the Civil War period.

Drawing room at Kenwood, home of Joel Rathbone, Albany, New York, illustrated in A. J. Downing, *The Architecture of Country Houses* (New York, 1850), fig. 179.

Center Table
Rosewood, rosewood veneer,
cherry, white marble

Attributed to Alexander J. Davis
(1803-1892)
New York City, ca. 1844
30 x 37 x 37 inches

VC-103

This remarkable table shows the craftsman's mastery of technique and materials. The hexagonal top and skirt are supported on a triangular base by a cluster of six free-standing columns executed in rosewood, a material used for the finest 19th century furniture. The austere geometric components have been embellished by an extensive use of curvilinear details. This manner of furniture is stylistically related to buildings illustrated by Andrew Jackson Downing, whose influential book, *The Architecture of Country Houses*, was published in 1850. According to family tradition, the table descended in the family of Joel Rathbone of Albany, New York, and it presumably is the table seen in an illustration from Downing's book (see page 18).

Cabinet
Rosewood, rosewood veneer,
mirror

Alexander Roux (1813-1886)
New York City, 1856-1866
90 x 46 x 23½ inches

1982.311

The massive lower portion of this
cabinet provides a striking
contrast to its delicate étagère.
The top is flanked by beautifully
carved scrolls, devices which are
repeated as sculptural relief on
the drawers and mirrored doors.
A printed trade card on the
cabinet's back gives the address
of Roux's shop, 479 Broadway,
where it was located from 1856 to
1866. One of New York's leading
cabinetmakers at mid-century,
Roux produced both elaborate
and simple furniture designs in a
variety of styles throughout his
career of nearly half a century.

Side Chair
Oak

Alexander Jackson Davis
(1803-1892)
New York City, ca. 1845-1850
39 x 18¼ x 20 inches

1981.1000.46

The designs of architect A. J. Davis are among the earliest examples of American furniture of a predominantly Gothic character. On this diminutive chair, the shaping of the back crockets on the crest is from the Gothic design vocabulary and the cloven hooves are from Classical design. These features are combined in new ways and the chair conveys a lightness not associated with Gothic furniture. An almost identical chair is in the collection of the Museum of the City of New York, a gift of Davis's son. Two drawings of this design survive.

Pitcher and Goblet
Silver

Zalmon Bostwick
(working 1845-1852)
New York City, ca. 1845
Pitcher: 11 x 8½ x 5½ inches
Goblet: 8 x 3⅞ x 3⅝ inches

VC-099.1, VC-099.2

Marked "Z Bostwick" and "New York," this pitcher has a presentation inscription on the base reading "John W. Livingston / to / Joseph Sampson / 1845." John W. Livingston (1804-1885), a descendant of 17th century settlers in New York City and in the Hudson Valley, had a distinguished naval career and retired as a rear admiral. Sampson was Livingston's son-in-law. Zalmon Bostwick lists himself in the *New York Mercantile Register* of 1848-1849 as the successor to William Thompson located at No. 128 William Street. He announced that he made "silver cups, urns, vases, etc." and was capable of "the manufacture of SILVER WARE, in all its branches: embracing Plain, Chased and Wrought." American silver in the Gothic mode is rare. This set originally was *en suite* with a matching pitcher and goblet now in The Brooklyn Museum. The pitcher is related stylistically to a stoneware pitcher, ca. 1838-1845, modeled by Daniel Greatbach for the American Pottery Company of Jersey City, NJ. Both American pieces were inspired by contemporary English ceramic models.

23

Rococo Revival

Perhaps the most exuberant of all mid-century high styles was the Rococo Revival. Although reinterpretation of this 18th century ornamental style began as early as the 1830s in France and England, Rococo decoration and form were not fashionable in this country until the 1850s. In the furniture of John Henry Belter and Alexander Roux, both of New York City, the style was characterized by robust forms, usually embellished with intricately carved decoration. By the Civil War, sophisticated taste had turned to other 18th century and Renaissance modes of decoration, but elements of the Rococo continued to appear well into the 20th century.

Pair of Ewers
Silver

Samuel Kirk (1793-1872)
Baltimore, 1830-1846
16⅝ x 9⅞ x 6½ inches

1982.302.1, 1982.302.2

Samuel Kirk was one of the most successful and influential American silversmiths of his day. Born in Doylestown, Pennsylvania, he was apprenticed to Philadelphia silversmith James Howell. By 1815 Kirk had completed his apprenticeship and had established a partnership in Baltimore with John Smith that lasted until 1820. The firm became Samuel Kirk and Son in 1846, when Henry Child Kirk joined his father's business. Since both ewers are marked "S. Kirk," they can be dated before 1846. In 1861 two other sons joined the company and its name was changed to Samuel Kirk and Sons. Samuel Kirk is best known for his extensive use of overall repoussé work, and he has been credited with the 19th century revival of this technique in the United States. The effect was often referred to as the "Kirk" or "Baltimore" style. The ornate 18th century silver produced in Philadelphia and Baltimore provided prototypes for this 19th century work.

Pier Table and Etagère
Rosewood, poplar, mirror

Attributed to Alexander Roux
(1813-1886)
New York City, 1850-1857
86½ x 79¼ x 29½ inches

1981.1000.66

This masterpiece of American
Rococo Revival furniture can be
attributed to the fashionable
cabinetmaker Alexander Roux
on the basis of an almost identical
example bearing this firm's label
in The Metropolitan Museum of
Art. The bold massing of the
table and the vigorous carving on
its upper shelves recall the broad
range of French decorative
arts—from the *Régence* as well
as from all the 18th century
Louis styles. The most
flamboyant of all mid-century
design revivals, the Rococo was
at that time referred to as the
"modern French style." The
imperial court of Napoleon III,
which commissioned dazzling
interpretations of 18th century
French styles, provided the
design source for this
particularly rich manifestation of
the Rococo Revival in the United
States.

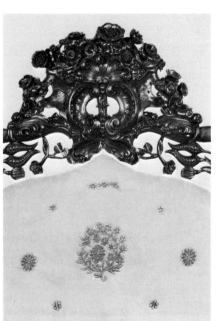

Sofa and Four Side Chairs
Laminated rosewood, white pine, ash, gilt brass castors, original appliqué designs on silk plush velvet

Attributed to John Henry Belter (1804-1863)
New York City, ca. 1855
Sofa: 51½ x 91¾ x 38½ inches
Chair: 39⅞ x 19⅛ x 27½ inches

1981.1000.61 - 1981.1000.65

Born in Germany, John Henry Belter came to New York City in 1833. During his thirty-year career in this country, Belter introduced a number of new furniture forms. Although his manufacturing process and

designs were technically progressive, Belter's furniture was finished by hand, as seen in the superb carving of these pieces. Belter received four patents protecting his inventions, the most important of which was a lamination process used in this suite. Thin layers of various woods were glued together at cross grains and bent under steam pressure in specially designed molds. These curved surfaces were then carved, perforated, and decorated. "Arabasket" was Belter's name for this pattern. The carved rosettes heighten the sculptural effect of each piece. Extensive parlor suites were popular in Belter's day, and this set was probably part of a much larger group.

27

French Classicism and the Louis Seize Style

During the 1850s, the *Ecole des Beaux Arts* in Paris was a major training ground for American architects and designers. One result was a revival of American interest in French 18th century classicism. Unlike the flamboyant Rococo Revival, French Classicism—and its interpretation in decorative arts, the *Louis Seize* style—was characterized by sobriety of form and decoration. The style found favor in relatively few households in the United States, however. Perhaps its delicacy of form and diminutive scale made this furniture seem unsuitable for the cavernous interiors of the sumptuous private houses constructed after the Civil War. A few fine examples survive, testimony to the original owners' demand for highly-developed craftsmanship.

Card Table
Rosewood, rosewood veneer, gilt incised lines, marquetry of lighter woods

Alexander Roux (1813-1886)
New York City, ca. 1867-1877
30¾ x 34¼ x 18 inches

1981.1000.43

The remarkable use of wood in the marquetry top of this card table attests to the skills of mid-19th century American cabinetmakers. The open grain of the wood swells gracefully around the geometric cartouche in the center of the top depicting card-playing equipage. The table's overall form is based on 18th century Neo-Classical English and Continental furniture. However, such robust interpretations of acanthus leaves above the fluting of the legs and the small geometric renderings of fans on either side of the Greek key freize on the skirt were commonly considered Neo-Grec ornament at the time of the Civil War.

Alexander Roux was one of the most important cabinetmakers working in New York at this time. In 1850, Andrew Jackson Downing praised his work: "In New York, the rarest and most elaborate designs . . . are to be found at the warehouse of Roux, in Broadway." Working in a variety of styles, Roux's name appeared in the New York City business directories from 1837 until the 1880s, first as an upholsterer and finally as a decorator. His work is characterized by strong design as well as superb craftsmanship. The paper label on the bottom of the table reads, "FROM / ALEXANDER ROUX, / 827 & 829 BROADWAY, / NEW-YORK. / French Cabinet Maker, / and importer of / FANCY & MOSAIC FURNITURE. / Established 1836." This helps to date the table, since Roux moved uptown to 827 Broadway in 1867 and then to 133 Fifth Avenue in 1877.

28

29

Desk and Bookcase
Ebonized cherry, poplar, maple, holly, white pine, ormolu mounts.

New York City, ca. 1865
70 x 52 x 23½ inches

1982.310

The prestigious partnership of Ringuet LePrince and his son-in-law, Leon Marcotte, advertised in an 1860 New York Evening Post: "very rich suites of Black Wood and Gilt . . . Black Center Tables with very rich Gilt Bronzes; elegant cabinets to match. . . ." This desk and bookcase, incorporating both gilt and patinated mounts, shows the technical mastery of this firm or one of its accomplished competitors. The piece is an early and robust interpretation of the *Louis Seize* style, a persistent and important 18th century design source for the late 19th century. The dynamic form and decoration are particularly strong. Flanking stencil-decorated niches for sculpture or vases were a 19th century convention, intended to promote art appreciation in the American home. Ebonized furniture originally purchased by Mrs. John Jacob Astor, now in the Preservation Society of Newport County, has similar elements of style and construction.

Pair of Vases
Porcelain, painted decoration, gilt
Paris, France, ca. 1865
VC-134.1, VC-134.2

Cabinet

Rosewood, rosewood veneer,
maple, ebonized trim, gilt
mounts and incised lines,
porcelain plaque, marquetry of
various woods

Thomas Godey (1820-1879)
Baltimore, 1867-1872
48 x 58 x 17 inches

1981.1000.41

This cabinet is among the most
important examples of
documented Baltimore furniture
from the second half of the 19th
century. Such elaborate pieces
are usually associated with New
York firms. The allegorical
symbols appearing in the
marquetry panels on the sides
and in the ceramic plaque
suggest that the piece was a
music cabinet. Its scale and
elegant materials would have
been appropriate for a music
room or parlor of a prosperous
household. The combination of
Louis XVI, Neo-Grec, and
Renaissance Revival detailing
parallels similar work at the
same time by such New York
makers as Alexander Roux. The
porcelain plaque was imported.

The label seen here is nailed to
the back of the cabinet. In 1850,
Thomas Godey succeeded John
Needles as one of the leading
cabinetmakers in Baltimore. In
1867, Godey moved his business
to 41 Hanover Street; in 1872,
his eldest son, Harry, joined the
firm and its name was changed to
Thomas Godey and Son.

Renaissance Revivals

In December 1887, the periodical *The Decorator and Furnisher* explained the term "renaissance" as embodying "the essence or nectar of the antique in new individual forms designed in responsive spirit to the true beauty of classical details, a blending of old art with new conceptions in structural compositions and its ornamental accessories. . . ." During the second half of the 19th century, arts of Renaissance Italy and France re-emerged as important design sources for the decorative arts. Initial references were general and tended to mix typical forms and decorations. Introduction of the style coincided with great technical advances in the manufacture of furniture. Large factories in eastern and mid-western cities popularized the style in simplified versions for bedroom and parlor sets. Large in scale, this style was appropriate for both public spaces and the spacious dwellings of post-Civil War America. Among manufacturers showing work at the 1876 Centennial Exhibition in Philadelphia, Renaissance Revival furniture was dominant. This style remained popular until the early 20th century.

THE EXHIBIT OF MESSRS. KIMBEL & CABUS.
THE CENTENNIAL—ART FURNITURE.—Photographed by the Centennial Photographic Company.—[See Page 970.]

Centennial Exhibition, illustration in *Harper's Weekly*, December 2, 1876, p. 969.

Piano
Ebonized cherry, bird's eye maple, ash, spruce, gilt, ivory

Hallet, Davis and Company (working 1850-1957)
Boston, ca. 1875
95 x 82½ x 31¾ inches

VC-115

Made for the 1876 Philadelphia Centennial Exhibition, this is one of the few surviving examples of major 19th century exposition furniture. Furniture made for the Exhibition enhanced the prestige of the manufacturer by showing his range of virtuoso skills. Using a Renaissance fireplace surround as a prototype, Hallet, Davis and Company replaced the mantelpiece with a keyboard. "Hallet, Davis & Co. / Boston. / PATENT." is painted above the keyboard. According to a contemporary account, "The superb piano . . . is undoubtedly the most elaborately constructed instrument of its kind at the Exhibition. . . . All of its handwork, the production of skillful carvers, . . . the panels, with their wreaths, scrolls, medallions, and symbolic figures, are elaborated with great fidelity of detail." Exhibition pieces are rare since their unusual size limited their market; presumably, they were broken up or reduced in size following the exhibitions. The black matte finish highlights the exquisite detailing and enhances the rich massiveness of the piano.

Cabinet
Walnut, maple, poplar, silk curtain

Daniel Pabst (1826-1910)
Philadelphia, ca. 1865
54 x 44 x 23½ inches

1981.1000.52

Daniel Pabst, one of the leading cabinetmakers in Philadelphia during the second half of the 19th century, learned his trade in his native Germany. Emigrating to America in 1849, he settled in Philadelphia, where he joined a community of German furniture makers that numbered about 725 in 1850. Although Pabst was one of many foreign-born workers with few connections, he became, according to a contemporary source, "one of the leading and most successful designers and manufacturers of artistic furniture in Philadelphia." Among his distinguished and wealthy clients was Beauveau Borie, whose monogram is incorporated in the central medallion. This cabinet was ordered for Borie's townhouse at 1035 Spruce Street, an imposing Italianate residence which still stands, though gutted by fire. The cabinet incorporates caryatid supports with finely-carved heads, characteristic of the high standards of Pabst's shop. The scaling on the top drawer and caryatids looks toward beaux-arts work at the end of the century.

35

Pair of Pedestals
(one illustrated)
Ebonized cherry, gilt

Probably New York City,
ca. 1875
42 x 25 x 16 inches

VC-109.1, VC-109.2

Ancient Egyptian ceremonial
pylons inspired the bold
architectural form of these
pedestals, which were probably
designed to hold portrait busts,
popular in 19th century interiors.
The incised gilt decoration and
the household function and scale
make these pedestals pure 19th
century creations.

Mantel Garniture
Marble, bronze, gilt, silver, glass, concrete

Retailed by Tilden, Thurber and Company (est. 1856)
Providence, ca. 1880
Clock: 17½ x 19⅜ x 6¾ inches
Obelisk: 27½ x 7 x 5 inches

VC-089

After the Civil War, mantel clock sets became popular. The French appear to have had a near monopoly on supplying mantel garnitures to Europe and America. Sold by such major American jewelry firms as Tiffany and Company of New York and J. E. Caldwell and Company of Philadelphia, these garnitures usually bear the name of the retailer. This set is inscribed "TILDEN THURBER & Co· / Providence" on the clock face. The installation of the obelisk in New York's Central Park in 1881 stirred interest in such ancient Egyptian motifs.

Armchair
Ebony, marquetry of ivory,
mother-of-pearl, lighter woods,
red pine

Probably New York City,
ca. 1875
38¾ x 26¾ x 35 inches

VC-056

This remarkable chair closely
resembles published work of
early 19th century designers
Thomas Hope, George Smith and
Pierre de la Mésangère. Their
Neo-classical work was
characterized by monumentality
and was frequently ornamented
with opulent detailing. This
particular chair, possibly
produced for an equally elaborate
interior, also exhibits
representational marquetry
similar to work executed by 18th
century German cabinetmakers
as well as Portuguese and
Spanish Colonial artisans. Both
this chair and its mate, which
was acquired by The
Metropolitan Museum of Art,
have the Kennedy family shield,
and were probably made as part
of a set for the library of Robert
Lenox Kennedy, a noted
bibliophile. Most of his collection
of books now forms part of The
New York Public Library.

Ewer
Porcelain, gilt, painted
decoration

Ott and Brewer
(working 1871-1892)
Trenton, NJ, 1876-1882
13¼ x 9 x 6⅝ inches

VC-096

This is a large and important
example of Ott and Brewer's
Belleek line. The firm applied
this name to several different
types of ceramics. This
egg-shaped ewer is ornamental
rather than useful; its elaborate
and complex design suggests that
the piece was made for an
international exhibition. Three
shades of gilding are used in the
elaborate decoration, which
combines Japanese themes.
Printed on the bottom is
"BELLEEK" above a crown and
sword, with "O & B" below. The
crown-and-sword mark was used
between 1876 and 1882.

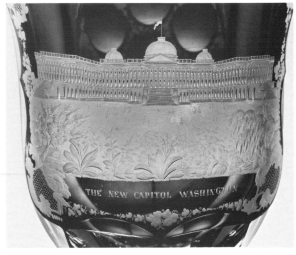

Vase and Cover
Clear and stained blown glass,
cut and engraved

Possibly manufactured by the
New England Glass Company
(working 1818-1888)
East Cambridge, MA,
ca. 1840-1860
19¾ x 7½ inches

VC-063

An article about the New
England Glass Company in the
Boston Transcript (June 16,
1852) reported: "We were
repeatedly struck with the fact
new to us that most of the
exquisite, richly colored and

decorated glassware which is so
much admired under the name of
'Bohemian Glass' is
manufactured at these works."
However, this evidence is not
conclusive, and it is equally
possible that glass with
American scenes could have been
made in Bohemia. The
engraving, which was probably
derived from a 19th century print
source, illustrates the Capitol
building before the construction
of its present dome. The
inscription reads: "THE NEW
CAPITOL WASHINGTON."

Chafing Dish
Silver

Gorham Manufacturing Company
(established 1831)
Providence, after 1865
7⅝ x 11½ x 10¼ inches

1982.305

Chafing dishes are relatively rare
in American silver, and this is a
superb example of Renaissance
Revival style. The finely cast
caryatid figures and drapery
festoons create a light openwork,
while the classical qualities make
the dish appear monumental. In
1831 Jabez Gorham formed a
partnership with Henry L.

Webster, creating Gorham and
Webster. In 1865 the firm
became Gorham Manufacturing
Company. Gorham
Manufacturing Company
exhibited at major international
expositions in America and
Europe. This piece is stamped
with the Company's trademarks
as well as "150 / S & M" and
"G484 / CH."

41

Punchbowl
Silver

Ball, Black & Company
(working 1851-1876)
New York City, 1865
13¼ x 12¾ x 12⅛ inches

1981.1000.57

This monumental punch bowl was presented to Charles Godfrey Gunther, mayor of New York from 1864 to 1866. A New York Times article of April 8, 1865, describes the occasion: "MAYOR GUNTHER was last evening presented by a number of his friends with a very handsome testimonial of their esteem in the shape of a silver punch bowl and fruit stand. The presentation took place at Delmonico's in Fourteenth Street." The arms of the City of New York and the State of New York are engraved on double medallions with a cartouche at the rim. "BALL BLACK & CO. / 985 / 1000 / NEW YORK" is stamped on the bottom of the bowl. Ball, Black & Company, along with Tiffany and Company, were New York's leading silver manufacturers in the second half of the 19th century.

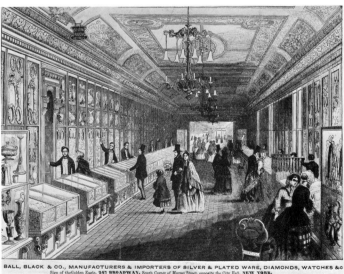

BALL, BLACK & CO., MANUFACTURERS & IMPORTERS OF SILVER & PLATED WARE, DIAMONDS, WATCHES &c
Sign of the Golden Eagle, 247 BROADWAY, South Corner of Murray Street, opposite the City Hall, NEW YORK.

This etching shows the interior of Ball, Black & Company, 247 Broadway, and is from the *Advertising Directory* of 1850. Photograph courtesy The New-York Historical Society.

42

Innovative Furniture

Ingenuity was an important dimension of 19th century furniture design and production in the United States. Samuel Pratt's 1828 invention of the spiral or coiled inner spring made possible sturdier, more cheaply manufactured, and more comfortable upholstered furniture. American innovation began to attract European attention, notably at the 1851 Great Exhibition in London, where Thomas Warren's Centripetal Chair was widely admired. With the expansion of national boundaries and improvement of transportation, portability became desirable and patents were issued for various types of folding furniture. Throughout the century, new materials and techniques of manufacture were introduced, and government patents were issued to protect the ideas of inventors and manufacturers from commercial theft and infringement.

Table
Reed, oak top

Wakefield Reed Chair Company
(working 1893-1895)
New York City, 1893-1895
29¼ x 25 inches

1982.313

Documented rattan furniture from the 1880s and 1890s is rare because of the fragility of the material. The flexibility of rattan enabled manufacturers to create flamboyant shapes seen in the C-scrolls and arches in the base of this table. Photographs of interiors of the period document the use of rattan furniture indoors as well as out. According to a source in the 1880s, one or two pieces of rattan were "indispensable in modern apartments." The close weave on the table is typical of reed and rattan furniture, which was widely popular until lighter wicker began to be used for the fanciful open forms of the 1890s. Attached to the bottom of the top frame support is a printed label reading "No. 3557 / MANUFACTURED BY / WAKEFIELD REED CHAIR CO. / NEW YORK."

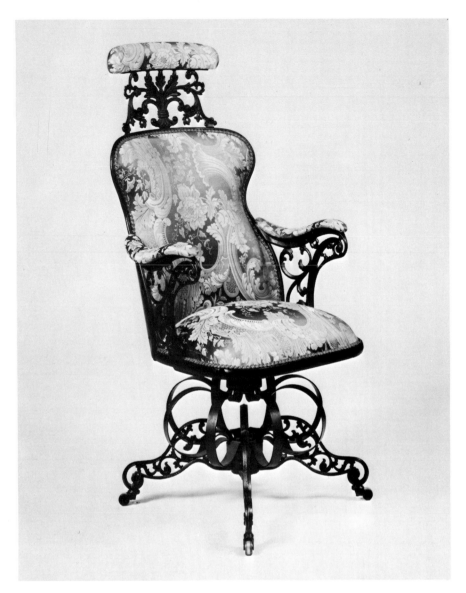

Centripetal Chair
Cast iron, steel spring, painted
sheet-metal back, 19th century
silk damask

American Chair Company
(working 1829-1858)
Troy, NY, patented
September 25, 1849
39¾ x 24½ x 30½ inches

VC-137

A remarkable invention in its
day, this revolving armchair is
supported by a center spring
patented by Thomas E. Warren
of Troy, NY, an ironmaking
center. Warren's spring device,
invented to enhance the comfort
of railroad travel, was
incorporated in domestic
furniture. This chair is an early
example of an American design
employing a cast iron frame for
seating combined with
upholstery and spring supports.
Displayed in several variations in
the 1851 London Crystal Palace
Exhibition, it was described in
The Illustrated Exhibitor: "The
framework . . . is wholly of cast
iron, the base consisting of four
ornamental bracket feet,
mounted on casters, and secured
to a center piece, to which eight
elliptical springs are attached.
. . . The freedom with which the
chair may be turned on its
center, renders it very
convenient to a person who may
want to turn to his library-shelf
or side table, as he can do so
without leaving his seat, . . . the
whole reflecting much credit on
the inventor and on American
Art."

44

Reclining Armchair
Oak

Theodore Hofstatter, Jr.
(working 1871-1914)
New York City, patented
August 30, 1881
40½ x 27½ x 32 inches

1982.314

This reclining chair is an American interpretation of the Morris chair, an 1866 English design by Philip Webb for Morris and Company. The chair is stamped twice on the back of the rear seat rail "THEO HOFSTATTER, JR. / PATENTED / AUG. 30, 1881." Hofstatter's chair received its patent because the reclining control was simpler "than the cumbersome and unsightly mechanism usually employed." Hofstatter entered business as a furniture manufacturer in 1871, succeeding his father. He is also credited with inventions of machinery for furniture construction.

Cast Iron Furniture

From the 1840s, cast iron garden furniture had widespread popularity in America. Development of coal mining in the United States made cast iron inexpensive to produce. Hutchison and Wickersham's 1857 *Descriptive Catalogue* listed a "Grape Settee," similar to the example by the John McLean Foundry, priced at $9 to $15. The bench and two chairs by Brown and Owen were based on an English pattern patented by Carron Company in Stirlingshire in 1846. This English patent, however, did not stop American foundries from producing identical and similar patterns. Because elements of cast iron furniture were made in expensive molds, patterns tended to be used over a long period of time, even into the 20th century. (The pattern of the Brown and Owen set was even reproduced in aluminum as late as 1957.) Without a foundry mark, cast iron furniture is difficult to date. Its prevalence in the second half of the 19th century, however, clearly makes furniture of this sort a document of taste for that period.

Bench
Cast iron

John McLean Foundry
(working 1884-1897)
New York City, 1884-1897
30¼ x 47 x 28 inches

VC-076

Bench and Two Armchairs
Cast iron

Brown and Owen,
ca. 1860-1900
Bench: 36 x 45 x 16½ inches
Armchairs: 35½ x 27 x 16½
inches

1981.1000.90, 1981.1000.91,
1981.1000.92

Chair
Cast iron

Probably New York City,
ca. 1860-1900
32 x 27½ x 21 inches

VC-074

Art Furniture and the Aesthetic Movement

The Aesthetic Movement began in England in the 1860s and reached the United States in the following decade. The movement's central conviction was that art was essential to the fulfillment of everyday life. Thus, ordinary objects required the careful attention an artist gave his art. Furniture, glass, and pottery, said the enthusiasts, deserved the same consideration bestowed on other art forms and merited contributions from established artists. What had been industry became fine art, and Art furniture, Art glass, and Art pottery were introduced. Idealistic theorists regarded the artisans who produced these wares as the heirs of centuries of time-honored traditions of craftsmanship. Before long, however, the commercial appeal of "Art" goods was usurped by mass-produced products, superficially similar to hand-crafted wares, made possible by new manufacturing techniques.

Exterior, Vanderbilt House
New York City, ca. 1882
Photograph from Strahan,
*Vanderbilt's House and
Collection*, Vol. 1

Parlor, Vanderbilt House
New York City, ca. 1882
Photograph from Strahan,
*Vanderbilt's House and
Collection*, Vol. 4

Side Chair
Maple, gilt, mother-of-pearl
inlay, 19th century Chinese
embroidered silk

Herter Brothers (working
1865-1908)
New York City, ca. 1881-1882
34½ x 16 x 16 inches

1982.316

Undulating lines and a
shimmering surface make this
chair a stunning evocation of
America's Gilded Age. This
unusual design, with its concave
and convex shapes, predates
American Art Nouveau by a
decade. Intended for William H.
Vanderbilt's Fifth Avenue
mansion, completed in 1882, this
chair was part of the furnishings
supplied by Herter Brothers, the
interior designers and architects
for the house. This chair appears
in photographs in Edward
Strahan's elaborate publication,
*Mr. Vanderbilt's House and
Collection* (New York, 1883-84).
The chair has been reupholstered
with a 19th century Chinese
embroidery similar to the
original.

49

Side Chair
Walnut, gilt, original upholstery

Probably New York City,
ca. 1870-1880
36 x 24 x 26 inches

VC-066

Combining a variety of
upholstery techniques and
fabrics in a harmonious
composition, this chair
documents the virtuosity of the
19th century upholsterer.
Innovations in springs and
upholstery made this chair
extremely comfortable—a major
concern of Victorian designers.
Although the upholsterer's art
reached new heights in the 1870s,
most of our knowledge of these
ingenious and luxurious creations
is supplied by photographs.
Because of the fragility of
textiles, few chairs have
survived in such remarkable
condition.

Side Chair
Mahogany, chestnut, marquetry
of mother-of-pearl and brass

Probably New York City,
ca. 1885-1890
38¾ x 17¼ x 19½ inches

1981.1000.58

The remarkable inlays of
mother-of-pearl and brass and
the precise carving on this chair
are distinctive features of this
example of Art furniture of the
late 19th century. The animal
heads carved at the top add an
exotic touch. Its maker is
unknown but this chair, though
delicate, has a commanding
presence and demonstrates a
craftsmanship worthy of the
most prestigious firms of the
period.

51

Bed
Rosewood, ebonized cherry, inlay of lighter woods, pine, brass

Herter Brothers (working 1865-1908)
New York City, ca. 1880
78 x 66 x 86 inches

VC-080

This bed is part of a suite which originally included a dressing table, armoire, bedside table, and several chairs. The set was ordered by Pierre Lorillard, possibly for his townhouse at 389 Fifth Avenue. An armoire from the set in the collection of the Toledo Museum of Art is inscribed "Lorillard" in pencil on the back and "Newport" in chalk on the base. Lorillard was a tobacco magnate, sportsman, and breeder of rare horses.

Veneered upon a decidedly "Eastlake" rectilinear form, the elaborate marquetry in the Japanese manner was a hallmark of Herter Brothers' custom work for a discriminating clientele. The Lorillard suite is related to several other bedroom suites made by Herter Brothers for affluent clients, including Jay Gould (The Metropolitan Museum of Art), William K. Vanderbilt (Biltmore House), William Carter (Philadelphia Museum of Art), and Collis Huntington (The St. Louis Art Museum). The bed is stamped "HERTER BRO'S" on each rail and slat. In pencil, "N 3202" and "Store" signify the Herter warehouse inventory number.

Cabinet

Rosewood, rosewood veneer,
American black walnut,
mother-of-pearl, brass, copper,
pewter

Herts Brothers (working
1872-1937)
New York City, ca. 1880-1890
59½ x 59¾ x 15¾ inches

VC-082

Until recently, Herts Brothers
was known to scholars mainly
through an illustration of their
Centennial bedstead and
directory listings. The skillful use
of materials and the fine technical
execution of this cabinet indicate
the work of a premier
manufacturer. Herts Brothers
was well known in its day,
displaying a completely furnished
bedroom suite at the Philadelphia
Centennial Exhibition.
Photographs and descriptions of
the library in William H.
Vanderbilt's Fifth Avenue
residence suggest that this
diminutive cabinet, stamped
"HERTS BROTHERS /
BROADWAY & 20STNY" on
the back, may have been made
for that room or its vestibule.
The piece is unusually low, which
would allow for the display of
objects on its top. Meticulous
attention to detail is most
apparent in the intricate inlay
work and engaged columns
flanking the glass doors. In
overall form and composition,
this piece is reminiscent of
French court pieces of the 16th
century, but its delicacy of
detailing, massing, and use of
materials are expressions of
rarefied late 19th century taste.

Cabinet
Ebonized cherry, marquetry of
lighter woods, gilt

Herter Brothers (working
1865-1908)
New York City, ca. 1880
60 x 33 x 16¼ inches

1981.1000.51

A balanced interaction between
surface ornament and form
makes this cabinet one of the
finest pieces by Herter Brothers,
New York's leading decorating
firm in the late 19th century.
Intricate and dramatic contrasts
of light and dark woods, gilding,
and ebonizing are highlighted by
the use of tinted metallic paints.
This superb example of cabinetry
shows the genius of Christian
Herter, one of the firm's
partners. His travels to Europe
and his exposure to Japanese
designs, as well as his passion for
painting, contributed to his
artistic vision. The firm's
customary mark, "HERTER
BRO'S," is stamped on the back.
A nearly identical cabinet,
executed in a lighter wood, is at
Sagamore Hill, Theodore
Roosevelt's Long Island summer
house.

54

Covered Vase
Earthenware, painted
underglaze decoration

John Bennett Pottery
(working 1876-1882)
New York City, 1876-1882
12 x 6⅜ inches

1982.287

According to Edwin Atlee
Barber's pioneering work, *The
Pottery and Porcelain of the
United States* (1909), John
Bennett was "formerly director
of the practical work in the
faience department of the
Lambeth pottery of Messrs.
Doulton and Company, of
London." Bennett was
responsible for painting the
Royal Doulton ware exhibited at
the Philadelphia Centennial
Exhibition. Bennett had come to
this country in 1876, settling in
New York City, where he
introduced his method of
decorating faience under the
glaze. The mark on this vase
indicates that it was made at his
first kiln, located at 101
Lexington Avenue. An 1878
edition of the American *Art
Journal* noted Bennett's efforts
in the United States, and called
his enterprise "a most valuable
and interesting Art-pottery
studio."

The striking design of orange
blossoms and fruit recalls textiles
and wallpapers by William
Morris (see page 66) and his
compatriots. This surface design
of nature motifs outlined by crisp
contour lines is characteristic of
English Reform theory and its
avoidance of three-dimensional
naturalism.

Vase and Stand
Glass, blown and molded

Hobbs, Brockunier and Co.
(working 1861-1889)
Wheeling, WV, after 1886
10 x 3¾ inches

VC-128

On March 8, 1886, the art collection of Charles Morgan was sold in New York City. Auction history was made by the purchase of a Chinese porcelain vase for $18,000 by Baltimore collector W. T. Walters, founder of the Walters Art Gallery. The vase was considered noteworthy not only for its high price, but also for its "graceful ovoid shape." Hobbs, Brockunier and Co. copied the shape of the famous vase in a colored glass called "Peach Blow."

Entree Dish and Cover
Silver

Van Sant and Company (working 1882-1886)
Philadelphia, ca. 1883
5¾ x 10½ x 6½ inches

1981.1000.59

Other than products of Gorham and Tiffany and Company, American silver in the Aesthetic taste is rare. Distinguished by superb craftsmanship and the application of Eastern details to a Western form, this dish is a compilation of decorative borders, including fans and cherry blossoms. The hexagonal motifs on the lid are borrowed from Chinese metalwork. It is possible that the designer of this piece was influenced by Japanese and Chinese work exhibited at the 1876 Philadelphia Centennial Exhibition.

According to the 1883 Philadelphia directory, John T. Van Sant & Co. was at 611 Sansom Street. The firm advertised as manufacturers and sellers of silverware. On August 18, 1886, the *Jewelers Weekly* reported, "John T. Vansant and Brother, manufacturers of silverware, Philadelphia, who have been in financial difficulties recently were sold out by the sheriff." The dish is marked "ENGLISH STERLING / 925-1000," with a pseudo-mark "V & Co." in a diamond. Two *en suite* dishes are in The Metropolitan Museum of Art and The Detroit Institute of Art.

57

Tray
Porcelain, gilt, painted
decoration

Ott and Brewer (working
1871-1892)
Trenton, NJ, ca. 1885-1890
15 x 16 x 3¼ inches

VC-093

Ott and Brewer was known for
Parian-ware busts of famous
Americans and historical figures,
exhibited at the Philadelphia
Centennial Exhibition. Later the
firm became known for its
Belleek line, first produced in
1882. The painted decoration on
this tray, executed in the
Japanese manner, resembles
published drawings by the
influential 19th century French
printmaker Félix Bracquemond
(1833-1914). Gilt and silver
representations of a bird, insects,
and plants, rendered in an
Oriental fashion, contrast with
the classical fluted shell form.
The tray is marked with the
initials of the manufacturer and a
crescent enclosing the word
"BELLEEK."

Late 19th Century Eclecticism

In the years between the 1876 Philadelphia Centennial Exhibition and World War I, the United States emerged as a major world power. Great fortunes were amassed by America's businessmen and industrialists, who constructed enormous mansions and commissioned artists and decorators to furnish them. Visionaries saw America as the newest and most promising society in the world, a new "Great Civilization," and applied the term "American Renaissance" to the period. In decorative arts, the term does not define a specific style, but suggests the wide range of design sources available to American architects and decorators and their affluent clients. If America was to be a new "Great Civilization," it seemed, it would create a new taste, assemble a new culture, by choosing from other civilizations. French châteaux in Newport, Italian palazzi in New York, and Colonial Revival townhouses in Boston represented attempts to recreate the best of the past. A taste for the antique became fashionable. Wealthy Americans considered themselves modern nobility, and surrounded themselves with 18th century French and Italian Renaissance furniture. When appropriate antiques could not be located, reproductions or adaptations were commissioned. Late 19th century interiors were visually complex, a sumptuous mix of furniture of various periods and styles.

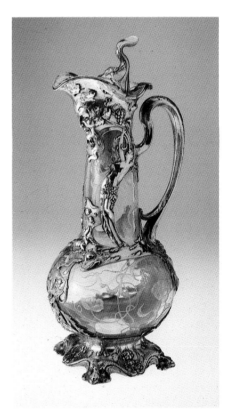

Claret Jug
Silver, glass

Gorham Manufacturing
Company (established 1831)
Providence, ca. 1900
13⅛ x 7 x 5⅞ inches

1982.306

Around 1895, Edward Holbrook, chairman of Gorham Manufacturing Company, together with Gorham's chief designer, the Englishman William J. Codman, decided to introduce a line called Martelé ("hammered"). Gorham trained craftsmen to create sinuous forms for the new line, working on individual designs so that each object might be considered a unique work of art. This claret jug is an unusual example of Gorham's line; it is noteworthy for its skillful combination of glass and silver. While executed in a variation of French Art Nouveau taste, the decorative theme of the ewer is a bacchanal, appropriate for a wine server. The bottom is stamped "SHREVE, CRUMP AND LOW," the Boston retailer. The Martelé line was first available in 1899.

Cabinet
Ebonized cherry, painted panels, glass

Will H. Low (1853-1932)
New York City, 1882
52 x 42 x 17½ inches

1982.320

The delicacy of the pastoral scene with idealized maidens contrasts with the bold architectonic massing of this ebonized cabinet. The inspiration for this type of decorated furniture was a group of "illuminated" cabinets produced by William Morris and other leaders of the English Reform Movement. Such work was less common in the United States. This example is documented by both the artist's signature, Will H. Low, and the date 1882, on the lower left panel, the right corner of the right panel, and the lower corner of the front panel. A popular painter of the late 19th century, Low collaborated with John La Farge on interiors, including the New York City residence of Cornelius Vanderbilt, II.

61

Library Table
Oak, aspen, gilt

Probably New York City,
ca. 1892
29 x 41⅜ x 70¾ inches

VC-132

American industrialists, with notions of Renaissance patronage, collected antique furnishings of that period and commissioned historically accurate reproductions of Renaissance furniture. The table shown here was owned by Cornelius Vanderbilt, II, and was probably commissioned when his townhouse at 1 East 57th Street in New York City was remodeled by George B. Post in 1892-93. Post had designed the house when it was originally built (1879-82), and he or one of his contemporaries with strong academic training may have designed this table. The Vanderbilt house was considered one of the most important commissions of its day. Leading artists and craftsmen—including Augustus St. Gaudens, John La Farge, Will H. Low, and Louis C. Tiffany's Associated Artists—were employed in its interior design and decoration.

Dressing Table
Maple, mahogany and
mother-of-pearl marquetry, pine,
brass rail, silver-plated pulls,
beveled mirror

Attributed to George A.
Schastey (working 1870-1897)
New York City, ca. 1880
86⅜ x 36 x 18¾ inches

1982.315

This dressing table is very
similar to the furnishings of the
dressing room designed for
Arabella Worsham Huntington's
house at 4 West 54th Street in
New York City. The house, as
remodeled by Mrs. Huntington,
was sold, furnished, to John D.
Rockefeller. In a letter to
Rockefeller on January 24, 1884,
New York cabinetmaker and
decorator George A. Schastey
wrote that he had been
responsible for the furnishing of
the house. The dressing table
represents the opulent yet
restrained Renaissance style in
America during the late 19th
century. Through Rockefeller's
generosity, three rooms from
Mrs. Huntington's house have
survived: two at the Museum of
the City of New York and one at
The Brooklyn Museum.

63

Covered Vase
Earthenware, gilt, painted
decoration

Faience Manufacturing
Company (working 1880-1892)
Greenpoint, NY, ca. 1886-1892
15⅜ x 10⅝ x 7¾ inches

1982.286

In 1880, the Faience
Manufacturing Company of
Greenpoint, Long Island,
initiated a line of pottery
decorated with hand-modeled
flowers. Many of these pieces
were designed by Edward
Lycett, who emigrated to this
country from Staffordshire,
England, and, beginning in 1861,
conducted an extensive business
in New York. In 1884, he joined
the Faience Manufacturing
Company and "at once set to
work to compound better bodies
and glazes and to design new
shapes and decorations, and soon
began the manufacture of richly
embellished pieces. . . ." He also
introduced a fine grade of
porcelain which combined the
characteristics of a faience and
the superior glaze of hard
porcelain. Lycett left the
company in 1890 and shortly
thereafter moved to Atlanta,
where he died in 1909. The
covered vase bears the conjoined
initials "FMCº" and the number
"1121."

Pitcher
Blown glass, painted enamel
decoration

Mt. Washington Glass Company
(working 1869-1894)
New Bedford, MA, ca. 1890
11⅜ x 5¼ inches

VC-068

Decorated white opal glassware
was produced by 18th century
English and continental
manufacturers, but it was not
until the late 19th century that
this ware was made in the United
States. White opal glass blanks
were matte-finished with an acid

bath, then decorated with exotic
designs in colored enamels. On
this pitcher, subtly-rendered
flowers are combined with
beading in a graceful and
vigorous design. Although the
irregular ribs of the handle may
have been meant to prevent
slippage, this pitcher was
primarily intended for decoration
rather than use. On a circular
paper label affixed to the bottom,
"CROWN MILANO / MT
W.G. CO." surrounds the firm's
insignia. Crown Milano, patented
in 1886, was one of Mt.
Washington's most popular lines
of art glass.

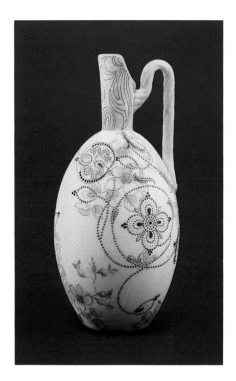

Vase
Blown glass, enamel decoration

Mt. Washington Glass Company
(working 1869-1894)
New Bedford, MA, patented
February 27, 1894
13⅜ x 7½ inches

VC-067

The complicated techniques
required to produce the Royal
Flemish line attest to the
capabilities of one of America's
foremost glass manufacturers.
Although the patent for
decorating this glassware line
was not issued to Mt.

Washington Glass Company
until 1894, wares were advertised
as early as 1889, and this vase
may predate the patent. The large
vase incorporates Moorish
decorative motifs in an
asymmetrical composition
typical of the late 19th century.
Distinguished by its subtle color
scheme and fine craftsmanship,
this important vase is
documented by the letters "R"
and "F" painted on the bottom
and a circular paper label with
"Mt. W.G. Co. PAT. APPLIED
FOR" and a double-headed eagle,
the firm's trademark.

Fabric Panel
Wool

William Morris (1834-1896)
London, England, after 1878
86½ x 32 inches

VC-097

The ideals and designs of William Morris had considerable impact on American designers at the turn of the century. Morris advocated a "simplicity of eye, begetting simplicity of taste," yet his fabrics and wallpapers were rich and complex. Though he was an active socialist who espoused a sharing of the arts, his firm's designs were luxurious, affordable only by the wealthy. Representations of birds frequently appeared in Morris's work. This fabric was introduced in the late 1870s as a result of research he conducted in the South Kensington (now Victoria and Albert) Museum's textile department. This pattern, entitled "Peacock," was executed in heavy twill and was often used for upholstery.

Tea Service
Silver, gilt, amethyst

Tiffany and Company
(established 1837)
New York City, ca. 1903
Teapot: 11 x 6 x 4¾ inches
Creamer: 3¾ x 4¾ x 3¾ inches
Bowl: 4¾ x 5½ x 4¾ inches
Sugar Tongs: 4¼ x 1½ x ⅝ inches
Tray: 16½ x 11⅜ x ¾ inches

VC-135

This opulent tea service is remarkable for the complexity of its decorative techniques and materials. Repoussé, gilt, enamel, and inset amethysts have been incorporated in an Islamic-inspired design of great originality. Islamic influence was apparent in the company's silver from the 1870s. The practice, in contemporary Russian enameled silver work, of integrating semi-precious stones was also a design source for Tiffany pieces of this period. Tiffany and Company showed a set similar to this one at the 1902 international exhibition in Turin, Italy. The set is marked "TIFFANY + Cº / 15557 MAKERS 5180 / STERLING SILVER / 925-1000 / C." The "C" mark indicates that the tea service was made while Charles T. Cook was president of Tiffany and Company, from 1902 to 1907. The pattern number "15557" indicates a date of 1903.

Vase
Blown glass

Tiffany Studios (working 1902-1932)
Corona, Long Island, NY, ca. 1902-1910
Trademark registered February 9, 1904
7½ x 5⅜ x 5⅜ inches

VC-075

Tiffany imbued this classic vase form with vitality, using rich coloration and dynamic convolutions related to European Art Nouveau. The soft iridescent luster was employed in much of Tiffany Studios' glass of this period, marketed under the name of Favrile Glass. This trade name is found on the paper label along with the registered Tiffany trademark of "LCT."

Arts and Crafts

After almost a century of rapid advancement in American furniture manufacture, some designers, under the guiding spirit of Gustav Stickley and others, advocated a return to sturdy hand-construction and "honest craftsmanship." Stickley rejected "showy" mass-produced furniture of the 19th century; his products were well-crafted and were usually made of oak. Methods of construction were clearly apparent in the finished work, with use of mortise-and-tenon joints as well as peg construction. Promotion of this simplicity in order to purify American taste was Stickley's goal. The Arts and Crafts Movement gained momentum at the turn of the century, and craft shops were founded across the country. The movement's influence extended into metalware, ceramics, printing, and bookbinding. Shortly after Stickley's introduction of "craftsman" furniture, American manufacturers realized that such goods could be mass-produced even more cheaply than simplified versions of Art furniture. While some of the Arts and Crafts potteries established as part of the movement continued producing until almost the middle of the 20th century, Stickley's accomplishments were largely ignored after World War I.

Vase
Pottery, glazed decoration

Paul Revere Pottery
(working 1908-1942)
Boston, after 1908
5⅞ x 4⅜ inches

1982.288

In the early 20th century, the Saturday Evening Girls, a group of young immigrant women in Boston, met weekly for reading and craftwork. The group's patron, Mrs. James F. Starrow, encouraged the founding of a pottery to be operated by the women, and, after the purchase of a small kiln, production began in 1908 in Brookline, Massachusetts. The pottery soon moved to Boston and was renamed the Paul Revere Pottery because of its proximity to the Old North Church. Most of the ware produced was decorated with incising and soft mineral colors incorporating stylized floral motifs. Supported by patrons, the pottery was not a money-making venture. In 1915, the operation moved to Brighton, Massachusetts. The pottery closed in 1942. While some of the decorators seem to have initialed their works—a conjoined "AM" and "S.E.G." are painted on the bottom of this vase—no record of identification has been located.

Plate
Porcelain, colored slip glaze

University City Pottery
(working 1910-1914)
University City, MO, 1914
9¼ inches diameter

VC-094

Located in suburban St. Louis,
the University City Pottery
employed leading artists of
Europe and America. In 1909,
Taxile Doat, who had worked at
Sèvres, joined the pottery.
American artists included
Adelaide Robineau and
Frederick Rhead. The first kiln
in University City began
operation in 1910. Using native
material, the pottery produced
high-fired porcelain with
crystalline glazes. The technique
of *pâte-sur-pâte* decoration, here
in a Virginia creeper motif, was
one of Doat's specialties. The
plate is marked with Doat's
monogram and the studio mark,
"UNIVERSITY CITY MO 1914
PORCELAIN WORKS."

70

Vase
Porcelain, crystalline glaze

Adelaide Alsop Robineau
(1865-1929)
University City Pottery
(working 1910-1914)
University City, MO, 1910
8⅝ x 3⅛ inches

VC-110

Adelaide Alsop Robineau's experiments in pottery and porcelain gave her an international reputation in her own lifetime. She was highly regarded for her crystalline glazes, applied to unusual forms like this small vase. Her porcelains received the Grand Prize at the International Exposition in Turin, Italy, in 1911. The vase was made while Robineau was working at the University City Pottery with her mentor, Taxile Doat, who had come to the pottery from Sèvres. Besides teaching, Robineau was editor of *Keramic Studio*, a national monthly publication. On the bottom of the vase is an incised cypher of conjoined "AR" in a circle surrounded by incised "1910," "123," and "UC."

Vase
Glazed semi-porcelain

Louis Comfort Tiffany
(1848-1933)
New York City, ca. 1904-1919
9⅞ x 4½ inches

VC-090

Louis Comfort Tiffany's glass and ceramic entries in the international expositions of the late 19th and early 20th century were critically acclaimed and influenced many avant-garde European artists and designers of the period. His use of new materials and innovative techniques established him as a leader in international design. This piece is from a line which Tiffany registered with the U.S. Patent Office in 1905. The vase was cast from a mold and then worked by hand. Its open wall construction indicates that it was intended for display rather than use. The floral components are more than decorative detailing; they define structural form. The ivory flow of glaze, concentrated in the recesses, emphasizes the relief of the hollyhock shapes without additional colored glazes. This subtle manipulation of materials is characteristic of Tiffany's approach to design. This vase is marked "LCT" on the bottom.

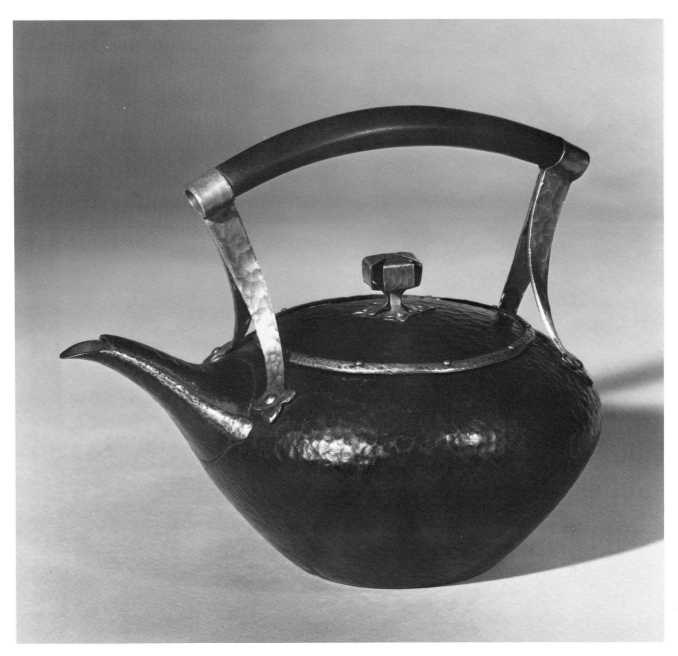

Teapot
Wrought iron, silver, ebonized
wood handle

Tiffany and Company
(established 1837)
New York City, ca. 1902-1907
6 x 7½ x 6 inches

1982.307

This small teapot, with its simple
elegant form and delicate
mounts, has great aesthetic
impact. The teapot's hammered
surface, the work of an individual
craftsman rather than mass

production, relieves the austerity
of the design. The pot is marked
"TIFFANY & CO. /
MAKERS / SILVER AND /
OTHER METALS / C / 1½
PINTS." The "C" mark dates
the pot between 1902 and 1907,
when Charles T. Cook was
president of the company.

Vase
Glazed earthenware, painted decoration

Newcomb College Pottery
(working 1895-1930)
New Orleans, ca. 1904-1910
12¼ x 7½ inches

1981.1000.56

In some American colleges and settlement houses in the early 20th century, shops were established to train young women in a craft. One of the most enduring of these was the pottery at Sophie Newcomb College, the women's affiliate of Tulane University in New Orleans. Here the young women decorated pots which had been thrown by professional potters, including Joseph Meyer (and for a brief time, George Ohr). This vase, thrown by Meyer, was decorated by Anna Frances Simpson. Painted on the bottom is the decorator's mark: "AFS DI DO-15." Impressed on the bottom are the cypher of an "N" within a "C" (for the Newcomb College Pottery), a conjoined "JM" (Meyer), and a "K." The most common decorative motifs on Newcomb College pottery were plants, animals, and landscapes indigenous to the South and especially to the bayou country around New Orleans.

Lamp
Glazed earthenware, leaded glass, bronze, teak

Grueby Faience Company (working 1894-1911), Boston Tiffany Studios (1902-1932), New York City, after 1902 23 x 15⅞ inches

VC-107

Collaborative efforts between artists and manufacturers in the late 19th and early 20th century resulted in a number of successful designs. The base for this lamp, which was also available as a vase, was designed by George P. Kendrick of the Grueby Faience Company in Boston, while the leaded glass shade is by Tiffany Studios. Grueby often collaborated with Tiffany Studios in the production of lamps.

William H. Grueby established the pottery in Boston in 1894 after training at the Low Art Tile Works in Chelsea, Massachusetts. At its peak, the pottery employed over 100 persons, and a separate division manufactured the art pottery. Although bankruptcy was declared in 1908, the pottery continued in production until the end of the 1920s. The base has an impressed mark on the bottom with a paper label reading "GRUEBY-POTTERY-BOSTON-U-S-A-REGISTERED TRADEMARK."

Rug
Wool

Retailed by Gustav Stickley's
Craftsman Workshops
Probably India, ca. 1910
73 x 76 inches

VC-112

Gustav Stickley's Craftsman
Workshops designed rugs with
bold geometric patterns which
were then made in India for the
American market. These rugs
provided a foil to the solid
furniture which Stickley's
Workshops produced. The
published catalogues of
Stickley's furniture included
these rugs, and similar rugs were
advertised in *The Craftsman*,
which Stickley published
between 1901 and 1916. The
magazine promoted Stickley's
philosophy and designs, and was
aimed at the growing American
middle-income market.

Hall Bench
White oak, brass

Gustav Stickley's Craftsman
Workshops (working 1900-1916)
Eastwood, NY, ca. 1910
31 x 47½ x 25¼ inches

VC-100

Gustav Stickley, this country's most vociferous opponent of mass-produced furniture, vigorously promoted the Arts and Crafts Movement and helped lead the development of a modern aesthetic in the United States before World War I. Stickley's early training was in a cabinetmaking shop. During an extended trip to England and Europe, he admired progressive design ideals of simplicity and honesty. After returning to America in 1898, Stickley incorporated many of these avant-garde concepts into his furniture. The designs he produced until his bankruptcy in 1915 exhibit a strict adherence to the straight line and the use of oak. Although hall benches appear frequently in renderings of Stickley-approved interiors, they were rarely included in his catalogues. The flat-paneled back indicates that this bench was designed to be placed against a wall. A red decal on the lower left of the back seat panel reads "Als / lk / kan / Gustav Stickley."

Architects and Designers

Architects have often been designers of furniture. At mid-19th century, Andrew Jackson Davis and Thomas U. Walter designed furniture for the buildings and interior spaces they created. In the last quarter of the century, some architects departed from the customary practice of employing and adapting historical styles and motifs. Frank Furness of Philadelphia used stylized, sometimes nearly abstract, forms from nature in decorating his buildings and furnishings. Frank Lloyd Wright dictated and designed interior fittings for his commissions, maintaining a conceptual unity of structure and furnishings.

Dining room of Theodore Roosevelt, Sr.'s home, New York City.

Table

Oak, chestnut, butternut, ash

Frank Furness (1832-1912)
Philadelphia, ca. 1876
26¼ x 66 inches

VC-072

One of the most imaginative American architects of the last half of the 19th century was Frank Furness, who was responsible for several important buildings in the Philadelphia area. Like other architects of the period, Furness often designed furniture. Many of his groups of free-standing and built-in pieces were manufactured by Daniel Pabst. For this table, commissioned for the New York City residence of Theodore Roosevelt, Sr., at 6 West 57th Street, Furness created a lively pedestal, finishing its corners with vigorous sculptural images of egrets and frogs. These vibrant but disciplined forms indicate Furness's awareness of works by sophisticated European designers. Pabst, one of Philadelphia's leading furniture-makers (see page 34), listed Theodore Roosevelt, Sr. as one of his clients, and Roosevelt family correspondence confirms the Furness-Pabst collaboration in the design and fabrication of the table. The table was inherited by Roosevelt's granddaughter, Alice Roosevelt Longworth, the daughter of President Theodore Roosevelt.

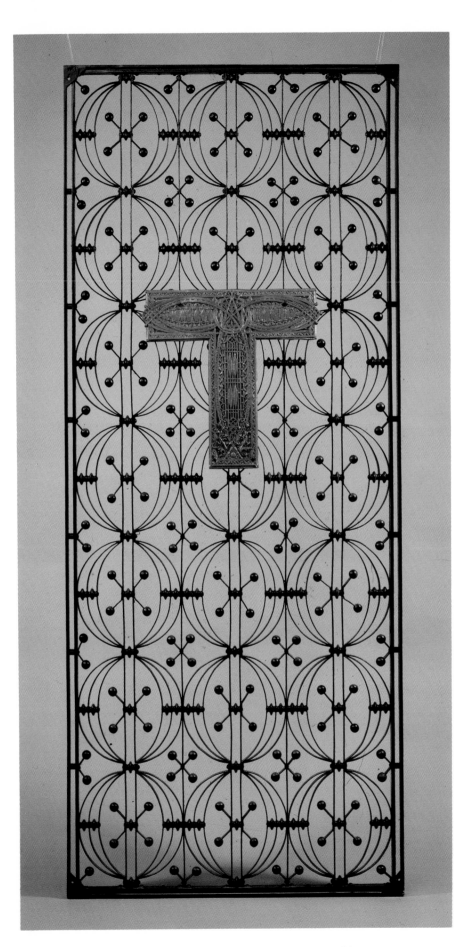

Elevator Grille
Bronze-plated cast iron

Louis Sullivan (1856-1924)
Chicago, ca. 1893-1894
73 x 31 inches

1982.291

Long before the 1893 Chicago Stock Exchange was demolished in 1972, a number of architectural elements were removed for remodeling, including this elevator grille with its lintel and T-shaped decorative plate. Originally part of a large bank of elevators, the grille shows the sort of conventionalized ornament favored by Louis Sullivan, the building's architect. Although the ornament was in a vocabulary Sullivan learned from the Philadelphia architect Frank Furness, the designs of Sullivan and George Grant Elmslie, master draftsmen in the firm of Adler and Sullivan, were original, and relied on few historical precedents. When designing interiors for his buildings, Sullivan created what he called a "system of ornament" so that all interior decorations and functional elements were related not only to one another but to the scheme of the entire building.

Armchair
Oak

Frank Lloyd Wright (1867-1959)
Chicago, ca. 1902
56¼ x 23 x 20 inches

1981.1000.49

Frank Lloyd Wright, the leading Prairie School architect at the turn of the century, designed this chair for the Ward Willits house in the Chicago suburb of Highland Park. This piece evolved from chairs Wright created for his own dining room in 1895. His 1895 chairs had perfectly vertical stiles; the Willits chairs are more subtle, with slight flairs to the back, top and feet. Including furniture in the commission added considerable expense to the house, yet Wright felt it was essential to overall architectural unity.

Dining room of Ward Willits house, Highland Park, Illinois.

Classical

Covered Sugar Bowl
Pressed lead glass, attributed to Providence Flint Glass Company, Providence, ca. 1831-1833, 5½ x 5 inches. VC-122

Andirons
Brass, iron, gilt, New York City or Philadelphia, ca. 1840-1860, 19¾ x 8⅞ x 16 inches. VC-083

Bottle
Blown and molded glass, Zanesville region, OH, ca. 1830-1850, 8¾ x 5½ inches. VC-129

Ewer
Silver, Stephen Richard (working 1815-1829), New York City, ca. 1825, 14¼ x 9⅜ x 6¼ inches. 1982.300

Gothic and Elizabethan Revivals

Gothic and Elizabethan Revivals

Armchair and Side Chair
Rosewood, birch, wooden casters, 19th century English needlepoint upholstery, New York City, ca. 1850, armchair: 45⅛ x 23½ x 24 inches, side chair: 40⅛ x 17 x 17¼ inches (not illustrated). 1982.309.1, 1982.309.2

Mantel, Grate, and Surround
Ebonized black walnut, pine, marble, cast iron, New York City, ca. 1845-1855, 51 x 56 x 9¼ inches. VC-069

Armchair
Oak, Alexander J. Davis (1803-1892), New York City, ca. 1857, 39 x 18¼ x 20 inches. Designed for John Herrick, "Ericstan" or Herrick Castle, Tarrytown, NY. 1982.317

Solar Lamp
Glass, brass, marble, attributed to the New England Glass Company (working 1818-1888), East Cambridge, MA, ca. 1855-1865, base: 15¾ x 5½ inches, globe: 18½ x 8 x 14½ inches. VC-081

Mantle Garniture
Bronze, gilt, marble, glass, William F. Shaw (working 1845-1890), Boston, patented December 18, 1848, candelabra: 16⅛ x 17¼ x 4 inches, candlesticks: 13¾ x 5¾ x 3¼ inches. VC-070.1, VC-070.2, VC-070.3

Rococo Revival

French Classicism and Louis Seize Revival

Rococo Revival

Pitcher
Glazed porcelain, gilt, William Boch and Brother (working 1845-1862), Greenpoint, NY, after 1853, 7⅝ x 6½ x 4½ inches. Inscription: "Meine Tochter / Anna / Von / Franz Hoppe." 1982.285

Pitcher
Porcelain, glazed interior, Fenton's Works, Bennington, VT, ca. 1847-1849, 10 x 8½ x 6½ inches. VC-104

Pitcher
Glazed earthenware, American Pottery Company (established 1833), New York City or Jersey City, NJ, ca. 1840-1845, 8¼ x 9½ x 5⅞ inches. VC-085

Pitcher
Molded earthenware, Rockingham glaze, Edwin Bennett Pottery (1844-1908), Baltimore, ca. 1850, 10¼ x 11¼ x 8¾ inches. VC-086

Table
Oak, gilt, marble, George Platt (1812-1873), New York City, ca. 1855, 35¾ x 29 x 16¾ inches. VC-091

French Classicism and Louis Seize Revival

Side Chair
Ebonized cherry, gilt mounts, casters, probably New York City, ca. 1865-1879, 36¼ x 23¼ x 26½ inches. 1981.1000.48

Sofa (not illustrated)
Rosewood, birch, 20th century reproduction upholstery fabric, attributed to A. and H. Lejambre (working 1865-1878), Philadelphia, ca. 1870, 47¼ x 73 x 33 inches.
VC-092

Armchair
Ebonized cherry, gilt mounts, casters, probably New York City, ca. 1865-1870, 38 x 30 x 32¾ inches.
1981.1000.47

Renaissance Revivals

Tall Clock
Walnut, walnut veneer, glass, gilt, bronze, Gustave Herter (working 1854-1865), New York City, ca. 1857-1865, 70¾ x 26½ x 16¼ inches.
VC-101

Armchair
Ebonized cherry, 19th century upholstery fabric, New York City, ca. 1870, 31½ x 28 x 26 inches.
VC-087

Armchair
Oak, leather, Thomas U. Walter (1804-1887), manufactured by A. Bembe and A. Kimbel, New York City, ca. 1857, 39 x 24 x 27 inches. Designed for the United States House of Representatives.
1981.1000.50

Sofa
Walnut, walnut veneer, pine, ash, attributed to John Jelliff and Company (working 1843-1890), Newark, NJ, ca. 1870, 46¾ x 78 x 33 inches. VC-116

Pitcher
Bisque porcelain, glazed interior, Karl Müller, manufactured by Union Porcelain Works (working 1862-1912), Greenpoint, NY, ca. 1876, 8½ x 6½ x 4¼ inches. VC-113

Mantel Garniture
Brass, bronze, gilt, retailed by J. E. Caldwell and Company (established 1848), Philadelphia, ca. 1865-1875, candelabra: 35½ x 11¾ x 11¾ inches, clock: 29 x 19 x 9¾ inches. VC-064.1, VC-064.2, VC-064.3

Cruet and Stopper
Blown glass, engraved by Louis F. Vaupel (1824-1903), manufactured by the New England Glass Company (working 1818-1888), East Cambridge, MA, ca. 1860-1870, 13 x 4½ inches. Descended in the family of Louis Vaupel. 1982.290

Ewer
Silver, Bigelow Bro. & Kennard (working 1845-1863), Boston, ca. 1860, 14⅜ x 7½ x 6⅜ inches. 1982.303

Innovative Furniture

Invalid Chair
Iron, painted decoration, cane seat and back, Cevedra B. Sheldon (working 1873-1877), manufactured by the Marks Adjustable Folding Chair Company (working 1877-1897), New York City, patented February 1, 1876, 46 x 29⅞ x 25½ inches. VC-130

Platform Rocking Chair
Reed and rattan, Ordway Chair Company (working 1894-1911), Framingham, MA, 1894-1911, 42 x 31½ x 25 inches. VC-139

Folding Chair
Walnut, ebonized and gilt, needlepoint, George Hunzinger (1835-1898), New York City, patented February 6, 1866, reproduction needlepoint, Harriet P. Neal, Atlanta, 38 x 24¼ x 35 inches. 1982.312

Cast Iron Furniture

Pair of Urns (not illustrated)
Cast iron, painted, gilt, J. W. Fiske (working 1864-1923), New York City, after 1875, 72 x 56 x 45 inches. VC-088

Art Furniture and the Aesthetic Movement

Vase
Stoneware, Isaac Broome (1835-1922), manufactured by Ott and Brewer (working 1871-1892), Trenton, NJ, 1876, 17¾ x 10¼ x 8¼ inches. 1981.1000.60

Ottoman
Rosewood, rosewood veneer, ash, marquetry of lighter woods, cedar, Herter Brothers (working 1865-1908), New York City, ca. 1882, 16½ x 19 x 16⅝ inches. 1981.1000.42

Clock
Brass, glazed ceramic tile, New Haven Clock Company (working 1853-1956), New Haven, CT, tiles manufactured by Low Art Tile Works (working 1878-1907), Chelsea, MA, ca. 1884, 12¼ x 6 x 9¾ inches. VC-105

Side Chair
Rosewood, rosewood veneer, marquetry of mother-of-pearl and lighter woods, brass stringing, chestnut, probably New York City, ca. 1885-1890, 36½ x 19½ x 18½ inches. 1981.1000.45

Armchair
Rosewood, rosewood veneer, marquetry of mother-of-pearl and lighter woods, brass stringing, chestnut, probably New York City, ca. 1885, 35½ x 32½ x 28 inches. 1981.1000.44

Vase
Glazed porcelain, applied porcelain decoration, Lotusware line, Knowles, Taylor, and Knowles (working 1854-1898), East Liverpool, OH, ca. 1892-1895, 8¼ x 6¾ x 5⅝ inches. VC-106

Vase
Silver, copper, turquoise, Tiffany and Company (established 1837), New York City, ca. 1900, 7½ x 8¾ x 9 inches. Exhibited at the Paris (1900) and Pan-American (1901) Expositions. VC-138

Late 19th Century
Eclecticism

Late 19th Century Eclecticism

Side Chair
American sugar maple, leather, G. Viardot, probably France, ca. 1890-1910, 36½ x 15 x 18½ inches. 1982.318.1

Book Plates (see page 48)
Photographs and photogravures, Edward Strahan, *Mr. Vanderbilt's House and Collection*, Holland Edition, published by George Barrie, Boston, 1883-1884. VC-114

Table
American sugar maple, G. Viardot, probably France, ca. 1890-1910, 29⅜ x 26¼ x 16¼ inches. 1982.318.2

Covered Box
Enamel on copper, Tiffany Glass and Decorating Company (1872-1902), Corona, Long Island, NY, ca. 1898-1902, 1¾ x 4 inches. VC-079

Vase
Silver, Tiffany and Company (established 1837), New York City, ca. 1881, 17¾ x 5 x 4¼ inches. VC-102

Table
Mahogany, birch, yellow poplar, beech, probably Eastern United States, ca. 1890-1910, 30¾ x 60 x 35½ inches. 1982.319

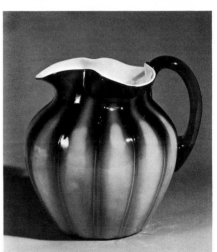

Vase
Enameled blown glass, gilt, New England Glass Company (working 1818-1888), East Cambridge, MA, patented 1886, 5⅛ x 5¾ inches. VC-136

Vase
Blown glass, Agata line, New England Glass Company (working 1818-1888), East Cambridge, MA, ca. 1885-1888, 8¼ inches. VC-133

Tankard
Silver, Gorham Manufacturing Company (established 1831), Providence, 17 x 8¼ x 7⅜ inches. 1982.304

Pitcher
Blown glass, Peachblow line, Hobbs, Brokunier and Co. (working 1861-1889), Wheeling, WV, ca. 1885-1889, 7 x 7¼ x 6¼ inches. VC-120

Pilgrim Vase
Semi-porcelain, acid-etched vellum finish, transfer print decoration, Chesapeake Pottery (working 1881-1889), Baltimore, ca. 1886, 18½ x 12¼ x 5½ inches. VC-077

Pitcher
Blown glass, Plated Amberina line, New England Glass Company (working 1818-1888), East Cambridge, MA, patented June 15, 1886, 7 x 7½ x 6¾ inches. VC-121

Arts and Crafts Movement

Vase
Glazed earthenware, Vasekraft line, Fulper Pottery (working 1860-1935), Flemington, NJ, ca. 1915, 13 inches. VC-117

Vase
Earthenware, luster glaze, Theopholis Brouwer (working 1894-1946), Long Island, NY, ca. 1900, 3¾ inches. VC-118

Vase
Earthenware, matte glaze, Van Briggle Pottery Company (working 1901-1920), Colorado Springs, CO, ca. 1902, 3⅞ x 2¾ inches. VC-095

Vase
Earthenware, painted decoration, Marblehead Pottery (working 1904-1936), Marblehead, MA, ca. 1880-1915, 6¾ x 4 inches. VC-065

Vase
Earthenware, matte glaze, Grueby Faience Company (working 1894-1911), Boston, ca. 1899-1910, 7¾ x 4½ inches. 1982.289

Plate
Glazed earthenware, painted decoration, Dard Hunter, manufactured by the Buffalo Pottery Company (working 1901-1956), Buffalo, NY, ca. 1910, 10 inches. VC-071

Vase
Earthenware, painted decoration,
Maria Longworth Nichols
(1849-1932), Cincinnati, ca. 1880,
17½ x 9⅛ inches. VC-078

Box with Lid
Copper, enamel, felt interior, Arts
Craft Shop, Buffalo, NY, 1905,
4¾ x 9 x 6¼ inches. VC-131

Vase
Glazed earthenware, Chelsea
Keramic Art Works (working
1872-1889), Chelsea, MA, ca. 1879,
7⅞ x 4¾ inches. VC-123

Pair of Lanterns
Copper, leaded glass, Karl Kipp,
manufactured by The Tookay Shop
(working 1912-1915), East Aurora,
NY, 1912-1915, 11½ x 5½ inches.
VC-073.1, VC-073.2

Runner
Wool, retailed by Gustav Stickley's
Craftsman Workshops (working
1900-1916), probably India, ca. 1910,
209 x 38¼ inches. VC-111

Side Chair
Oak, leather, Charles Rohlfs
(1853-1936), Buffalo, NY, ca. 1900,
46½ x 19¾ x 22½ inches. VC-022

Screen
Oak, leather hinges, Charles Rohlfs
(1853-1936), Buffalo, NY, ca. 1900,
each panel 72 x 22¼ inches.
1981.1000.53

Architect-Designed Furniture

Cabinet
Oak, brass and glass, Art Crafters, Cincinnati, ca. 1915, 58 x 28 x 12 inches. VC-108

Sideboard
White oak, oak veneer, hammered copper mounts, Gustav Stickley's Craftsman Workshops (working 1910-1916), Eastwood, NY, ca. 1910, 48¾ x 66 x 23¾ inches. VC-098

Tile
Glazed earthenware, Low Art Tile Works (working 1878-1907), Chelsea, MA, ca. 1879-1883, 9½ x 8⅛ inches. VC-124

Architect-Designed Furniture

Desk
Cherry, brass, leather, Leopold Eidlitz (1823-1906), manufactured by Weller, Brown and Mesmer, Buffalo, NY, ca. 1879, $29^{1}/_{16}$ x 26½ x 23¾ inches. Designed for the Assembly Chamber, New York State Capitol, Buffalo. VC-127

Lamp (not illustrated)
Bronze, leaded glass, Chicago, ca. 1915, 22½ x 24 inches. VC-119